AMELIA AND

STORY BY PAM MUÑOZ RYAN

ELEANOR GO FOR A RIDE

BASED ON A TRUE STORY

SCHOLASTIC PRESS

NEW YORK

PICTURES BY BRIAN SELZNICK

The author and illustrator gratefully thank the Amelia Earhart
Birthplace Museum in Atchison, Kansas; the Associated Press; Mark
Renovitch at the Franklin Delano Roosevelt Library at Hyde Park;
Mary Ternes and Matthew Gilmore at the Martin Luther King
Memorial Library (Washingtoniana Division); Kristine Anthony and
Brian Nicklas at the National Air and Space Museum (Archives
Division); the White House Curator's Office; and the White House
Historical Association.

The photograph on page 40 is printed courtesy of the National Air
and Space Museum, Smithsonian Institution. Photo number 87-2489.

LIBRARY OF CONGRESS CATALOGING-IN-PUBLICATION DATA
Ryan, Pam Muñoz
Amelia and Eleanor go for a ride / by Pam Muñoz Ryan; illustrations
by Brian Selznick.   p.   cm.
Summary: A fictionalized account of the night Amelia Earhart flew
Eleanor Roosevelt over Washington, D.C., in an airplane.
ISBN 0-590-96075-X (alk. paper)
1. Earhart, Amelia, 1897–1937—Juvenile fiction. 2. Roosevelt,
Eleanor, 1884–1962—Juvenile fiction. [1. Earhart, Amelia,
1897–1937—Fiction. 2. Roosevelt, Eleanor, 1884–1962—Fiction.]
I. Selznick, Brian, ill. II. Title.   PZ7.R9553Am   1999
[Fic]—dc21   98-31788

Printed in Mexico   49
10 9 8 7 6 5   0/0 01 02 03
First edition, October 1999

The illustrations in this book were drawn with graphite pencil and
colored pencil. The display type was hand lettered by Paul Colin based
on Brian Selznick's designs. The text type was set in 18 point Cooper
Oldstyle Demi Bold. Book design by David Saylor

To Lisa, Tonia, and Christina,
in loving memory of
Socorro Muñoz Kimble,
their courageous mother.
— P. M. R.

To Tracy Mack
— B. S.

AMELIA AND ELEANOR were birds of a feather.
Eleanor was outspoken and determined.
So was Amelia.
Amelia was daring and liked to try things other women wouldn't even consider.
Eleanor was the very same.
So when Eleanor discovered that her friend Amelia was coming to town to give a speech, she naturally said, "Bring your husband and come to dinner at my house! You can even sleep over."

It wasn't unusual for two friends to get together. But Eleanor was
Eleanor Roosevelt, the First Lady of the United States, who lived in
the White House with her husband, President Franklin Roosevelt.

Amelia was Amelia Earhart, the celebrated aviator who had been the first female pilot to fly solo across the Atlantic Ocean. And when two of the most famous and adventurous women in the world got together, something exciting was bound to happen.

In a guest room at the White House, Amelia and her husband, G. P., dressed for dinner. Amelia pulled on the long white evening gloves that were so different from the ones she sometimes wore while flying.

Many people didn't understand why a woman would want to risk her life in a plane. But Amelia had said it more than once: "It's for the fun of it." Besides, she loved the feeling of independence she had when she was in the cockpit.

She carefully folded a gift for Eleanor—a silk scarf that matched her own. The powder blue with streaks of indigo reminded Amelia of morning sky.

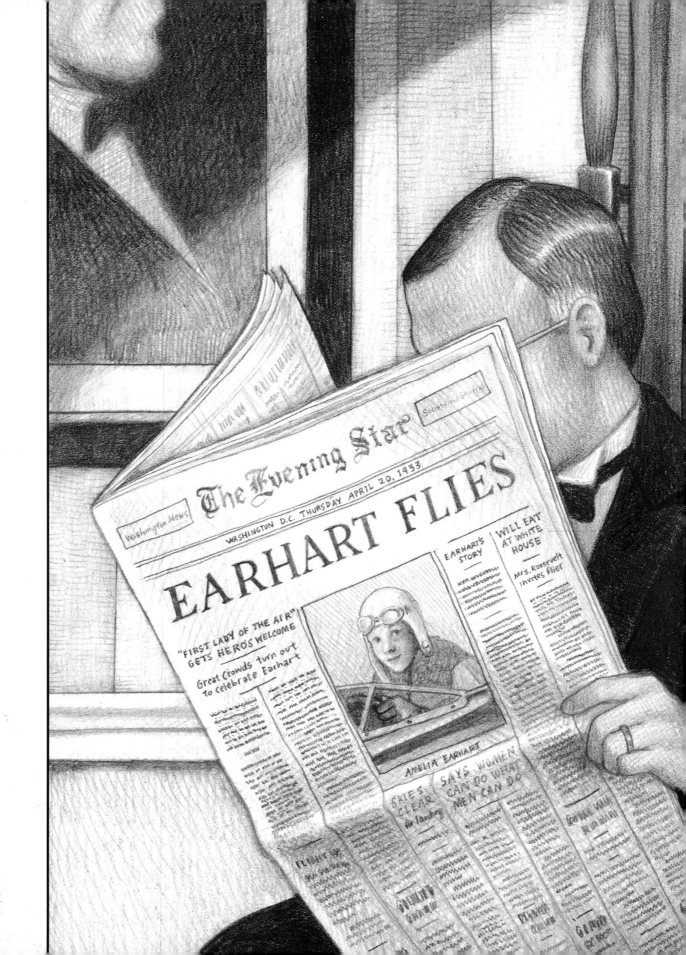

Meanwhile, Eleanor dressed for dinner, too. Her brother, Hall, would be escorting her this evening because the President had a meeting to attend. But Eleanor was used to that.

She pulled on the long white evening gloves that were so different from the ones she sometimes wore while driving. Then she peeked out the window at the brand-new car that had just been delivered that afternoon. She couldn't wait to drive it.

Many people thought it was too bold and dangerous for a woman to drive a car, especially the First Lady of the United States. But Eleanor always gave the same answer: "It's practical, that's all." Besides, she loved the feeling of independence she had when she was behind the wheel.

It was a brisk and cloudless
April evening. The guests had
gathered in the Red Room, and
the table looked elegant, as even
small dinner parties at the White
House can be.

Eleanor and Hall greeted
Amelia and G. P., as well as
several reporters and a
photographer.

Amelia gave Eleanor the scarf.

"I love it!" Eleanor exclaimed.
"It's just like yours."

Dinner started with George Washington's crab chowder.

"This is delicious," said Amelia. "But if soup at the White House has such a fancy name, what will dessert be called?"

Perhaps Abraham Lincoln's peach cobbler? Or maybe Thomas Jefferson's custard? They laughed as everyone took turns guessing.

By the time they got to the roast duck, the conversation had turned to flying.

"Mrs. Roosevelt just received her student pilot's license," said one of the reporters.

Amelia wasn't surprised. She had been the one to encourage Eleanor. She knew her friend could do anything she set her mind to.

"I'll teach you myself," offered Amelia.

"I accept! Tell us, Amelia, what's it like to fly at night in the dark?"

Everyone at the table leaned closer to hear. Very few people in the whole world had ever flown at night, and Amelia was one of them. Amelia's eyes sparkled. "The stars glitter all about and seem close enough to touch.

"At higher elevations, the clouds below shine white with dark islands where the night sea shows through. I've seen the planet Venus setting on the horizon, and I've circled cities of twinkling lights."

"And the capital city at night?" asked Eleanor.

"There's no describing it," said Amelia. "You just have to experience it on a clear night, when you can see forever. Why, we should go tonight! We could fly the loop to Baltimore and back in no time!"

The Secret Service men protested. "This hasn't been approved!"

"Nonsense!" said Eleanor. "If Amelia Earhart can fly solo across the Atlantic Ocean, I can certainly take a short flight to Baltimore and back!"

Before dessert could be served, Amelia had called Eastern Air Transport and arranged a flight.

Within the hour, Amelia and Eleanor boarded the Curtis Condor twin-motor airplane. For a moment, both women looked up at the mysterious night sky. Then, without changing her gloves, Amelia slipped into the cockpit and took the wheel.

The plane rolled down the runway, faster and faster. Lights from the airstrip flashed in front of them. And they lifted into the dark.

"How amusing it is to see a girl in a white evening dress and high-heeled shoes flying a plane!" Eleanor said.

Amelia laughed as she made a wide sweep over Washington, D.C., and turned off all the lights in the plane.

Out the window, the Potomac River glistened with moonshine. The capitol dome reflected a soft golden halo. And the enormous, light-drenched monuments looked like tiny miniatures.

Soon the peaceful countryside gave way to shadowy woodlands. The Chesapeake Bay became a meandering outline on the horizon. And even though they knew it wasn't so, it seemed as if the plane crawled slowly through starstruck space.

Eleanor marveled, "It's like sitting on top of the world!"

When it was time to land, Amelia carefully took the plane down. A group of reporters had gathered, anxious to ask questions.

"Mrs. Roosevelt, did you feel safe knowing a girl was flying that ship?"

"Just as safe!" said Eleanor.

"Did you fly the plane, Mrs. Roosevelt?" asked one reporter.

"What part did you like best?" said another.

"I enjoyed it so much, and no, I didn't actually fly the plane. Not yet. But someday I intend to. I was thrilled by the city lights, the brilliance of the blinking pinpoints below."

Amelia smiled. She knew just how Eleanor felt.

As the Secret Service agents drove them slowly back to the White House, Amelia and Eleanor agreed that there was nothing quite as exciting as flying. What could compare? Well, they admitted, maybe the closest thing would be driving in a fast car on a straightaway road with a stiff breeze blowing against your face.

Arms linked, they walked up the steps to the White House. Eleanor whispered something to Amelia, and then they hesitated, letting the rest of the group walk ahead of them.

"Are you coming inside, Mrs. Roosevelt?" someone asked.

But by then, they had wrapped their silk scarves around their necks and were hurrying toward Eleanor's new car.

Without changing her gloves, Eleanor quickly slipped into the driver's seat
and took her turn at the wheel. With the wind in their hair and the brisk air
stinging their cheeks, they flew down the road.

And after they had taken a ride about the city streets of Washington, D.C.,
they finally headed back to the White House . . .

. . . for dessert! Eleanor Roosevelt's pink clouds on angel food cake.

Eleanor Roosevelt's Pink Clouds on Angel Food Cake

ANGEL FOOD CAKE

1 cup cake flour (sift before measuring)

1¼ cups egg whites (10 or 12)

1½ teaspoons cream of tartar

1½ cups sugar

1 teaspoon almond flavoring

¼ teaspoon salt

Sift flour at least twice. Beat egg whites with beater until foamy; add cream of tartar and 1 cup of sugar gradually. Continue beating until egg whites stand up in peaks. Add almond flavoring. Sift remaining ½ cup of sugar with salt and flour, and very carefully fold into egg whites. Bake in tube pan in 375 degree oven for 30 to 35 minutes.

WHIPPED CREAM AND STRAWBERRIES {PINK CLOUDS}

1 pint strawberries

½ pint heavy cream, whipped

½ cup sugar

Crush berries with sugar. Let stand 30 minutes. Carefully fold berries into whipped cream. Spoon on top of angel food cake.

Adapted from: THE PRESIDENTIAL COOKBOOK: FEEDING THE ROOSEVELTS AND THEIR GUESTS
by *Victoria (Henrietta) Nesbitt, White House Housekeeper, Doubleday, 1951.*

AUTHOR'S NOTE

Amelia and Eleanor. Just mentioning their names brings choruses of, "They're my heroes," or "I've always loved and admired them." So when I found an obscure reference to their night flight, I couldn't wait to write a story about it—if only it were true. I sat in the library and scanned rolls and rolls of newspaper film and finally found the Associated Press articles. Later, Brian Selznick found a photograph from that very evening. The incident really happened!

In 1932, Amelia Earhart did what was then considered unthinkable. She flew solo across the Atlantic Ocean to demonstrate that "women like to do such things, and can!" The world reacted with unbridled excitement. In addition to Amelia's flying achievements, she made her mark in other ways. In the 1930s, she disapproved of the special minimum-wage law for women, which was lower than that for men, and she fought for equal rights for men and women. After her famous flight, she was invited to speak at many functions where she discussed her political views as well as her experiences flying. In 1932, Eleanor Roosevelt was asked to introduce Amelia at one of these speeches. That's how they met.

Eleanor Roosevelt moved into the White House in 1933, during the Great Depression. She transformed the role of First Lady by becoming a commanding role model. When the country went on food rationing, she insisted that the White House do the same. When cars became increasingly popular, she drove one, despite criticism. When she saw inequality, she became an activist for women's and human rights. Her practical approach to issues gained her enormous respect. Many people have said she was a woman ahead of her time. She would have said it was just common sense.

Eleanor loved flying and did receive her student pilot's license with encouragement from Amelia, who intended to teach her. Eleanor sent the license to Amelia as proof that she was ready to begin her training, but Franklin discouraged the plan: They could not afford an airplane and it was a risk that he did not wish her to take. Eleanor agreed, but she continued to love and promote air travel. She flew more passenger miles in the 1920s and 1930s than any other woman in the world!

On April 20, 1933, Amelia and her husband, G. P. Putnam, were invited to spend the night at the White House. Amelia was in town to give a speech the next day to the Daughters of the American Revolution. That night, still in formal dresses and white gloves, Amelia arranged to take Eleanor for a flight over Washington, D.C.

Although Amelia did take the controls for part of the flight, the plane was also flown by two of Eastern Air Transport's pilots, due to regulations. For this fictionalized book, though, it seemed much more exciting to have these two good friends and brave women alone on this wonderful adventure. Eleanor did take a turn in the cockpit, where the pilot explained the controls to her, and when the plane took an unexpected dip, the reporters joked that the First Lady was flying it. Almost all of Amelia and Eleanor's dialogue in my story comes from newspaper accounts, book transcripts, and diaries.

Eleanor loved cars and driving. Some people said she liked to drive fast. Whether or not there was a new car waiting when she and Amelia got back from the airport remains speculative. One research account supports the story, and I loved the idea that they might have really sneaked away together.

Amelia herself recorded that they ate crab chowder that night for dinner. She mentioned it in her thank-you note to Eleanor, which I found during my research. And angel food cake was Eleanor's favorite dessert, a fact confirmed by *The White House Diary* and *The Presidential Cookbook*, both by Henrietta Nesbitt, the Roosevelts' housekeeper during their White House years.

Amelia Earhart and Eleanor Roosevelt were remarkable women who mesmerized the public with their lives. Sadly, in 1937, in an attempt to be the first woman to fly around the world, Amelia and her plane mysteriously vanished somewhere over the South Pacific. She was never heard from again.

In 1938, a year after Amelia Earhart's tragic disappearance, her husband, G. P., found Eleanor Roosevelt's student pilot's license among Amelia's papers. He wrote to Mrs. Roosevelt and enclosed the license as a memento of the time when Eleanor Roosevelt almost became Amelia Earhart's "star pupil."

Amelia and Eleanor look out the window of the Eastern Air Transport plane during their night flight on April 20, 1933.